# EVOLUTION OF MNCS (MULTI-NATIONAL CORPORATIONS) AS SUBJECTS OF INTERNATIONAL LAW

## VOLUME 2, ISSUE 2 OF BRILLOPEDIA

SAURABH AJIT DHOTE

# Contents

# Preface

"Start writing, no matter what. The water does not flow until the faucet is turned on".

-Louis L'Amour

Hundreds of students and professors are contributing their work to Brillopedia, we are here to provide ample information about Law and Contemporary issues. Our aim is to provide a platform for today's generation to express their views and ideas on law and contemporary law.

# Publication

This research paper is published in volume 2, Issue 2 of Brillopedia

• vii •

# Author

# CHAPTER ONE

# Abstract

MNCs are the driving engine of a nation. This paper is the study of Evolution of MNCs (Multi-National Corporations) as the subjects of International Law. MNCs were in operation since long but were not the subjects of International Law. MNCs were in existence since the British rule in India and other nations. British East India Company was an MNC founded in the year 1600. It was headquartered in England but operated in many countries. Another example of such MNCs is French East India Company. It clearly shows that the MNCs were in operation since 1600s. MNCs were not the subjects of International Law back then. Now MNCs are accepted as the subjects of International Law. There are many International Laws and Municipal Laws governing the working of MNCs. Indian Companies Act 2013 governs the working of MNCs. MNCs are the companies operating in more than one country. For the development of economy and for utilisation of good labour these companies function in more than one country. This gives them advantage of saving proportionate costs. This has also helped the nations in inviting innovations and development. MNCs have also helped in GDP growth. However, this paper also studies the legal challenges faced by the MNCs. When it comes to laws related to companies, they may vary from country to country. One of the biggest challenges is working of the courts in India. The procedure is archaic and judgement may take many years to be delivered. This can become an obstacle for the progress of MNCs in India. Problem of courts functioning can be tackled if proper reforms are implemented. In these cases, ADR (Alternate Dispute Resolution) can be extremely helpful in effective resolution of disputes. The rise of MNCs has been splendid over the last fifty years, some of the great of examples of MNCs are Reliance, Apple, Google, Tata Group, etc. This is the result of evolution. The growth of MNCs has benefitted to the humanity at large. MNCs have also been instrumental in solving global issues of transportation and communication. To regulate these MNCs law makers came up with plethora of rules and regulations. There have been certain famous disputes with respect to MNCs in India and all over the world. Henceforth, these corporations have become one of the important subjects of International Law. The primary objectives of this paper are, to study the MNCs as subjects of International Law, to gain the insights as to how MNCs were born, to study advantages of MNCs to the global economy, to study what legal challenges have been faced in case of MNCs as subjects of International Law and to study the solutions for solving the legal problems.

**Keywords-** MNC (Multi National Corporation), Economy, Proportionate Cost, Innovation, GDP (Gross Domestic Product), Transportation and Communication, ADR (Alternate Dispute Resolution), Courts

# CHAPTER TWO

# Introduction

International organisations are one of the most important subjects under international law. These organisations possess the international personality. The international laws apply to these organisations to the extent of rights and obligations. Previously such organisations were not the subjects of international law. Only the states were the subjects of international law. However, this created many challenges. For example, the representatives of such organisations were unguarded because no such rights and obligations were legislated. With the progress of international law, a need was felt to regulate these organisations. Now, the international organisations, individuals and MNCs are the subjects of international law.

MNCs (Multi-National Corporations) are the foundations of almost every economy. MNCs have been instrumental in country's growth. MNCs were not the subjects of international law.They were unregulated in the past. Consequence of this was monopolistic practices by the companies.But now they are accepted as the subjects of international law. International as well as municipal laws regulate the functioning of MNCs. Main purpose of making MNCs as subjects of international law was to establish fair market practices and regulate investments.

# CHAPTER THREE

# What are MNCs?

MNCs are the Internationational Non- Governmental Organisations (INGOs). They are international corporations, referred to as Multi-National Corporations. Examples include the Coca- Cola Company, Sony, Nintendo, McDonald's, and Toyota[1].

A multinational corporation is a centrally coordinated company that is established in more than one nation-state. A typical multinational corporation comprises a parent company in one state with subsidiaries in one or more other states[2]. These are also called as transnational corporations because they operate in more than one nation.

Hence, the prerequisite for an MNC is to be operating in more than one nation. Merely exporting of products does not make a company an MNC.

**Legal personality**

MNCs have legal personality. They are capable of possessing a legal personality as a separate legal entity. They are capable of entering into contracts. Corporations can enforce their rights through what is arguably the most robust enforcement system in international law.

Corporations often have a choice of venues in which they can seek enforcement, and generally need not exhaust domestic remedies[1].

[1]Internationational Legal Personality: How the Investment Law Answers the Supreme Court in Jesner, Just Security, available at https://www.justsecurity.org/45543/international-legal-personality-corporations-investment-law-answers-supreme-court-question-jesner/, last seen on 15/12/2021.

[1]M. P. Tandon, V. K. Anand, International Law and Human Rights, 328 (18th ed., 2017).

[2]Multinationational Corporations in International Law, Oxford Bibliographies, avalaible at https://www.oxfordbibliographies.com/view/document/obo-9780199796953/obo-9780199796953-0049.xml, last seen

on 15/12/2021.

# CHAPTER FOUR

# MNCs as Subjects of International Law

MNCs are the subjects of International Law. All the international laws apply to these corporations. Rights and duties are applicable to these organisations. MNCs possess the legal personality and can enforce its rights and they can also be held liable for the breach of its obligations. The human rights laws are also applicable to these corporations.

### History

One of the first Multinational Corporations in the world was East India Company. There were many such companies under this brand name. Such as British East India Company, French East India Company and Dutch East India Company, etc. The British East India Company was established in the year 1600. It was formed for trading purposes. These companies spotted the advantages of doing business in the east and Asian region. The company was formed to share in the East Indian spice trade. That trade had been a monopoly of Spain and Portugal until the defeat of the Spanish Armada (1588) by England gave the English the chance to break the monopoly. Until 1612 the company conducted separate voyages, separately subscribed. There were temporary joint stocks until 1657, when a permanent joint stock was raised[1].

Another such company was French East India Company. The French East India Company was formed in 1664 AD during the reign of King Louis XIV to trade with India. In 1668 AD the French established their first factory at Surat and in 1669 AD established another French factory at Masaulipatam[2]. This company was established with the main purpose of trading but eventually the policies of French changed and India was considered as a colony.

There were these two powerful companies working in India. Both considered India as their colony. There was a great tension in the country. A power struggle began. This led to Carnatic Wars. Carnatic Wars were the military conflicts between French East India Company and the British East India Company.

Finally, due to the revolt of 1857 the company's rule came to an end. Later that period India was ruled under British Crown.

It can be understood from the above instances that the world faced consequences because of these corporations not being the subjects of international law. Number one consequence was unfair competition. Some of these companies had monopoly over certain parts which severely affected the working of other businesses. Secondly, there was confusion with regards to compliance of laws because the laws of nations werealtogether different. Thirdly, there was a grave violation of Human Rights. Unfair labour practices were followed. There was no rule regarding working hours of the workers. Workers were exploited in various ways, such as non-payment of wages, excessive workload, and etc. Last but not the least the environmental damage. Many such companies were established solely for the purposes of exploitation of resources. This led to natural degradation. Setting up of factories created pollution and eventually the environment was damaged. These companies were not bound by any laws and hence, performed all acts as per their whims and fancies.

Therefore, after consideration of various viewpoints these corporations are subjects of the international law. The International Investment Laws and Human Rights Laws are applicable to the corporations. With the advent of globalisation, it was a necessity to declare corporations as the subjects of international law.

[1] East India Company, Britannica, available at https://www.britannica.com/topic/East-India-Company, last seen on 16/12/2021.

[2] Arrival of the French and establishment of French East India Company, Jagran Josh, available at https://www.jagranjosh.com/general-knowledge/arrival-of-the-french-and-establishment-of-french-east-india-company-1442914204-1, last seen on 16/12/2021.

# CHAPTER FIVE

# Functional Theory

There are primarily three theories with respect to subjects of international law viz, realist theory, fictional theory and functional theory. Realist and the functionaltheory take the two extreme opinions. As per the realist theory only the state is subject of international law and according to the fictional theory only the individuals are the subjects of international law. The functional theory conciliates these two theories. It is a practical theory based on dynamic nature of international law. It creates a balance between the two theories. In both the theories i.e., Realistic and Fictional adopted their opinion without considering other subjects of International law. But the functional theory tends to meet both the extremist theories. According to this theory neither Nation States nor Individuals are the only subjects of International law. Even, not only the Nation States and Individuals are the subjects of International law but other entities have been granted international personality and status and considered as Subjects of International law[1].

Functional theory is one of the most appropriate theories. It strikes a balance between two extreme theories. Nature of international law changes with time. It is a dynamic law. For tackling the current challenges, it is necessary to make the laws flexible. Hence, functional theory takes into consideration these challenges. Therefore, according to functional theory the MNCs are also the subjects of international law because the theory clearly mentions that even non state entities are the subjects of international law.

[1]Rohit Raj, What is International Law all about, iPleaders, available at https://blog.ipleaders.in/subjects-international-law/, last seen on 17/12/2021.

# CHAPTER SIX

# LPG (Liberalization Privatization and Globalization)

Till the year 1991 India was a 'closed economy'. There were many barriers to trade. Very few foreign companies could set up their businesses in India. One of the biggest hindrances was the policy of granting of licenses. Many businesses could not even procure the license for doing the business.

But with introduction of LPG (Liberalization Privatization and Globalization) India became the 'open economy'. The government announced a New Economic Policy on July 24, 1991. This new model of economic reforms is commonly known as the LPG[1]. This was the historical moment for Indian economy. It opened the gates of Indian economy. It enhanced the trade in the country. Most importantly MNCs started to set up their businesses in India. The legislature showed the green signal for entering India. This encouraged the global companies to start operating in our country. India is now a hub to many Multi-National Companies in the world.

[1]Introduction to LPG, Vedantu, available at https://www.vedantu.com/commerce/introduction-to-lpg, last seen on 17/12/2021.

# CHAPTER SEVEN

# Legal Framework

Indian Companies Act, 2013 regulates the functioning of MNCs in India. One of the key features of the act is that it encourages international mergers, either way i.e. a foreign organization merging into an Indian Company, and vice versa. However, such mergers would take place only after permission has been duly obtained by the RBI[1]. Examples of such mergers are Walmart and Flipkart. The act has made it flexible for the companies to be merged with foreign companies. SEBI regulations are applicable on all the MNCs in India.

[1]What are the salient features of Indian Companies Act, 2013?, Taxmann, available at https://www.taxmann.com/post/blog/709/what-are-the-salient-features-of-companies-act-2013/, last seen on 17/12/2021.

# The Challenge

The functioning of courts is one of the biggest challenges faced by MNCs in India. The procedure is archaic. Justice is delayed for many years. A huge number of cases are already pending in the courts. As many as 21,259 cases were pending before the National Company Law Tribunal (NCLT) as of December 31, 2020, and more than 2,270 cases were filed before the tribunal under the insolvency law in the first nine months of this fiscal, according to the government[1]. A study by PRS Legislative Research says that there are 4.5 crore pending cases across all courts in India, with nearly 9 out of 10 pending cases stuck in subordinate courts[2]. This is the issue for the MNCs. Already there are these huge pending cases and solving new cases has become more difficult. This creates problems for companies because it affects their future contracts. It also affects the further progress. Goodwill of the company is also tarnished. The Vodafone International Holdings v. Union of India[3] is a landmark judgement. The time taken for delivering this judgement is around 4 years. It becomes difficult for the companies to take further decisions. Progress is stalled. The problems with the Indian **judicial systems** arise because the pleadings system is archaic, and therefore most court proceedings require large volumes of paperwork since everything needs to be pleaded. Akshay says: "The result is a long-drawn-out system, and there's a lot of pressure in terms of volume of cases given that this is a country of 1.1 billion people. Trials can take more than 10 years to complete."[4] It is a herculean task for the companies to get the speedy justice. The administrative functioning is altogether a different challenge which adds to the burden on the companies.

[1]Over 21,250 cases pending before NCLT at end of December 2020, The Economic Times, available at https://economictimes.indiatimes.com/news/economy/policy/over-21250-cases-pending-before-nclt-at-end-of-december-2020/articleshow/80754041.cms, last seen on 17/12/2021.

[2]Tejeesh N. S. Behl, 4.5 crore pending cases, over 50% judges missing-why justice in India take so long?, TOI, available at https://timesofindia.indiatimes.com/india/4-5-crore-pending-cases-50-judges-missing-why-justice-in-india-takes-so-long/articleshow/87203443.cms, last seen on 17/12/2021.

[3]Vodafone International Holdings v. Union of India, [2012] 1 S.C.R. 573.

[4]Chris Parsons and Nimi Patel, India: Legal Issues Facing Multinational in India, mondaq, avalaible at https://www.mondaq.com/india/international-trade-investment/76898/legal-issues-facing-multinational-in-india, last seen on 17/12/2021.

# CHAPTER NINE

# Possible reforms

Many scholars and jurists have suggested this solution for the companies' facing issues of delayed justice. ADR (Alternate Dispute Resolution) is one of the best possible solutions for the resolution of company's disputes. There are certain advantages of ADR such as it is usually faster and less costly, people have a chance to tell their story as they see it, it is more flexible and responsive to the individual needs of the people involved, it is more informal, the parties' involvement in the process creates greater commitment to the result so that compliance is more likely, the confidential nature of the process, Alternative Dispute Resolution is more likely to preserve goodwill or at least not escalate the conflict, which is especially important in situations where there is a continuing relationship[1]. ADR is really helpful for speedy resolution of dispute. Speedy and fair resolution is the efficacy of ADR. There many elements under ADR. They are as follows-

1. Mediation
2. Negotiation
3. Conciliation
4. Arbitration

One best available mechanism can be mediation. Here the mediator sits between the two parties and listens to their contentions and gives the possible solutions for resolution of disputes. It is effective because it helps the parties to go in appropriate direction and get the disputes resolved in speedy and proper manner.

Negotiation is when both the parties sit together to solve the dispute themselves or through their representatives for example lawyers. Negotiation can be ineffective because the parties may not come to agreement for settling of dispute.

Conciliation is defined as an alternative dispute resolution mechanism that is designed to resolve a dispute among the parties through a non-adjudicatory and non- Antagonistic way. It involves the neutral third party who makes the disputant parties arrive at a conclusion and a satisfactory dispute settlement[2].

Out of all the mechanisms arbitration is one of the most preferred and effective form of mechanism. Almost every company contract involves an arbitration clause. The arbitration in India is governed by the Arbitration and Conciliation Act, 1996. Many provisions under this act are borrowed from UNCITRAL (United Nations Commission on Trade Law). Arbitration is effective in case of speedy resolution of disputes. It is also comfortable and easy for the parties to get the issues resolved quickly. There are one or more than one arbitrator who resolve the disputes by giving an arbitral award.

Apart from ADR there is a necessity for legal reforms for speedy delivery of judgements. Special provisions are required for speedy and fair delivery of judgements. Efficient functioning of NCLT and NCLAT is necessary. Effective working of courts will help the Multi-National Companies in making progress.

[1]Advantages of alternate dispute resolution, Legal Services, available at https://lawhandbook.sa.gov.au/ch27s10s01.php, last seen on 17/12/2021.

[2]Concept of conciliation and role of conciliator, VIA MEDIATION & ARBITRATION CENTRE, available at https://viamediationcentre.org/readnews/NjM2/CONCEPT-OF-CONCILIATION-AND-ROLE-OF-CONCILIATOR, last seen on 17/12/2021.

# CHAPTER TEN

# Conclusion

MNCs have played a very important role in the progress of society at large. It has boosted the economic progress of India. MNCs are one of the most important subjects of international law because they impact the functioning of the country. MNCs have been in existence since 1600s. Growth of MNCs since then is unprecedented. After implementation of LPG the growth of MNCs has been tremendous. The Indian Companies Act, 1956 was amended to encourage the setting up of MNCs in India. International Investment Law is applicable to all the MNCs. It governs the working of these companies at international law. There are certain challenges faced by the MNCs in India. But one of the biggest among those is the working of courts. Delays in delivery of judgement severely affect the functioning of MNCs. However, if the provisions regarding fast functioning of courts are implemented then it will help the MNCs to progress freely in our country.